The R.U.S.H. Revolution

Dyanne,

Wishing you a life full of choices that drive your life in a direction you choose and brings happiness.

R.U.S.H. oN - xo,

Jessie H. B.

Lyssa,

Wishing you a life
full of choices that drive
you life in a direction
of chasse and bring
happiness.

Austin - xo,
Lizzy B.

The R.U.S.H. Revolution

Revving Up Self-Happiness through the Power of Intentional Living

JESSIE HARRIS BOUTON (WITH PENNY JO VESCHUSIO)

ISBN: 0692793062
ISBN-13: 9780692793060
Library of Congress Control Number: 2016917150
Inwell Press, Rome, NY

This book is dedicated to

- *you, the reader, who, when purchasing this book, started creating your own personal R.U.S.H. revolution. You have the power to intentionally choose your Best Life Ever. By doing so, you will positively change the world; and*
- *my children, who are living examples of the positive culture and lifestyle I seek to inspire and who are the reason for all that I do.*

Contents

Acknowledgments

Just as in my racing days, when races were won because a team worked together, this book too is a team effort, its wisdom drawn from my life experiences and those of the people closest to me. Somehow I don't feel I could ever express the magnitude of grateful emotion that fills me as we take the win light with this book.

To my husband, Chris, and our three beautiful sons, Cruz, Tino, and Maximo: your support and love are my strength, and nothing is more important to me in my life.

To my mom, Penny, who saw the vision and embraced it and then went on to develop my chicken-scratch thoughts into an eloquently written inspirational book: I am grateful. You have offered so much value to the entire process. I'm proud to have you by my side every step of the way. A mother's love is priceless and precious. Thank you for always showing me the way.

To my stepdad, Joe; my sisters, Jillian, Marie, and Megan; and my father-in-law and mother-in-law, Sox and Sharyn: I've been truly blessed by all your love and encouragement over the years. Thank you for being all that you didn't have to be.

To my late father, Art, who is always in my heart and has been the inspiration for my total-wellness passion.

To my former racing-team owners, teammates, racetrack officials, and fans: because of you, I learned to embrace confidence and courage that I didn't know I had and then went on to share that same confidence and courage with others—and what's more, to help others build confidence and courage for themselves. I will always consider you my second family, and for as long as I live, I will probably tell you too often how much I love and miss you. The wonderful memories that we made together can never be replaced in my heart.

To my many friends and clients: you've changed my life. Thank you for trusting me to share my R.U.S.H. life concept with you.

Introduction

This book is about choices and changes. It's not about how to become an entrepreneur or an author or a race car driver, even though I have become all three. It is about how to make choices and sometimes changes in your everyday life that will allow you to experience your Best Life Ever!

All people own their life stories, but how odd it seems that most people don't understand or embrace the fact that they also *write* their life stories. They can be the heroes or heroines, or they can be victims. They can drive the car or ride in it. They can be whatever they want to be, or they can be whatever everyone else wants them to be. They are truly writing their own stories, whether they realize it or not, because of the choices that they make in their lives. We all make choices every day. Even when we don't make a decision about something, we have made the choice not to make a decision and therefore must accept whatever else may come to us as a result of that choice.

The key thing to remember about making choices is that when you make conscious choices about every aspect of your life, it means that you are living intentionally, and there is true power in that. *Big* power. Power enough to change your life and the lives of your family members to the extent that you feel fulfilled and grateful every single day. Living intentionally allows you not only to dream but also to achieve your dreams, whatever they may be. Living life with intention (proactively) versus living life on automatic and simply reacting to what each day brings to your doorstep (reactively) can make you the hero—the superstar—of your own life story. Yes, making a good decision is powerful, and it can change your life! But a word to the wise: a bad decision can change your life too. You live life only once, and there are no do-overs, so you should want to make it the best it can be.

As is the case with most stories that are about change, there must first be a reason to change—a motivator. Usually it comes down to identifying something that you don't want in your life and then determining how to make it better. That something might trigger an emotion in you that makes you stop in your tracks and say, "Enough. I don't want this in my life anymore. I don't have to stay this way. I need to make a change." It must be a strong enough emotion to make you declare, "I *will* make a change."

For some reason, it seems that we are more apt to make changes if they lessen some type of pain or emotion rather than just because we know they will be good for us. Maybe you don't want to be overweight anymore. Maybe you don't want to live paycheck to paycheck. Maybe you don't want to work in a particular workplace or be unemployed. Or maybe you don't want to feel the way you do around certain people in your life. My point is that if something pains you enough, it will motivate you to make a change.

We are also more apt to make changes if we are afraid that by not doing so we will lose something that brings us extreme pleasure. Whatever the motivator is for you, it takes clear identification of that current life status as well as identification of a desired life status in order to map out a plan for how to get there, how to actively make choices that will enhance your life.

My personal motivator, which I share with you in this book, launched me onto a new path of becoming a physical fitness and life coach as well as the owner of a health and wellness company. I founded Infinity Wellness Project, an online business that offers programs promoting a total wellness concept that encompasses body, mind, and soul and advocates personal and professional success through the power of intentional living.

My hope is that by sharing the story of my elevated awareness of the control we have in our own lives, I will be able to help you, the reader – a person just like me – to know that you are not alone in feeling that there must be more out there but being unsure how to find it. You're not alone when you feel self-doubt starting to creep into your day. Reading my story can help you find a way to make intentional, conscious choices about how to live your life so that it brings you the most self-happiness. I want to revolutionize how you think about your own happiness and the power of intentional living, and I want to inspire positive change in you and for you.

xxoo,

Jessie

"What's that?" she asked.

"It's a problem," the voice told her.

"Oh, it looked like an opportunity to me," she said, as she adjusted the glasses on the bridge of her nose.

One

The R.U.S.H. Revolution

"Not good enough." That was the thought that kept running through my mind, and that was the beginning of my own personal revolution. I had good health, a beautiful family, and a comfortable life. I had achieved past success as the winningest jet car driver in history, owned a successful business, and was a much loved wife and mother and a respected member of my community, but I had recently spent far too much time feeling stressed and tired and depressed. My natural tendency to doubt myself was starting to take over my life.

I, of all people, had gotten a bit lost in all the roles in my life, and I was suddenly aware that I needed to make a choice. The choice was either to accept this unhappy state as the new me and deal with it or to reject that state and say "not good enough." In other words, I had to choose between being unhappy and negative every single day or seeking out and creating a better life for myself in which I could be happier and in turn make my family's lives happier. I needed to "rev up my self-happiness"—a phrase I like to call *R.U.S.H.*—and I needed to take back my life. It was time for a R.U.S.H. Revolution!

Taking my life back meant that I first had to know what I wanted my life to be about. I had to determine what I felt was missing in my life and then determine what would make me happier. I was quick to realize that this task was larger and more complicated than it initially seemed. Life happiness requires a total wellness plan. Total wellness encompasses many different factors, and it isn't something that can be achieved overnight and never worked at again. Total wellness absolutely has to be a daily priority and a continual way of life.

That epiphany caused me to identify seven "infinity factors" that I believe are key to achieving true happiness by way of living life intentionally, living by choice and not by chance. If you plan it, it can happen. Right then I knew that this 300-mph race car driver, mom, and wife was about to become a 300-mph self-happiness champion who specialized in creating and claiming both business and personal success.

How we look at things in our everyday lives is the single most important factor that determines where we go, what we do, and how we feel about everything that happens in our lives. Whatever you tell yourself about who you are, what you can do, and who you can become is exactly what your future will hold.

There are plenty of scientific studies you can research to explain how all that works and why that is the case; I am not a scientist or a psychologist, however, and so I will not even attempt to speak about our physical wiring or the complexity of our brains. I want to speak to you just as an ordinary person who learned that people for generations have recognized the power of positive thinking. Those who used that piece of wisdom to their advantage were much happier and more content with their lives. I want to talk to you about the things I have witnessed and experienced in my life that I believe can apply to yours as well.

Everyone experiences problems or some type of unhappiness in life. I have had my share of problems, if you want to call them that. I much prefer to call them "situations" or "R.U.S.H. opps." Calling them something other than problems takes some of the negative connotation away, and that's important, because how we think about something has a direct effect on how we feel about it. How we feel about things determines how happy we are.

No one has to agree with you on what causes unhappiness in your life. Different people view different things as problems. Only you know what pushes your buttons and what means the most to you in your life. How you view those things, though, can be the very life-blood of leading your Best Life Ever. You need to put on new glasses and see your problems as opportunities to turn your life around.

Don't buy into the idea that life events control and dictate your level of happiness. If you don't like something in your life, change it. You can! You have the ability and the responsibility to take whatever you don't like and turn it into something more positive. This might sound overly simplistic to you, but I am here to tell you that it is not. Living a R.U.S.H. lifestyle takes discipline and practice, because the human condition and our society often convince us that we are powerless, but we don't have to be. I'll say it again: *we don't have to be powerless.* We just need to view our problems—our situations—as opportunities, as R.U.S.H. opps.

How do we do that? Some things are very hard to handle in life, and finding a positive in them can seem impossible at first.

When I was eleven years old, my father passed away. It hurt terribly. It was unfair, and I was angry and sad. At eleven years old, it was hard to see it as anything other than painful. Over time, though, I found that focusing on his death rather than remembering the good things we shared only hurt me more. I learned that I had an opportunity to remember him with love and to embrace my present life to move past the pain.

I was blessed with a loving and supportive family. My mother redefined her life and helped me redefine mine in a way that acknowledged the unfairness of it all yet helped me to see that life can go on. If I'm honest with myself, this is where my R.U.S.H. Revolution concept took root. It took me a long time to embrace it, but over the years, little by little, I started to view negative things not just as negative but also as opportunities to make something positive come from them.

It was a challenge to revolutionize my thinking and move beyond my emotions to a place of control. I think doing so will always be a challenge—after all, we're only human—but it is achievable. Some positive things that came from losing my dad at a young age included having a more realistic view of the world, understanding the need to cherish all relationships, and developing a commitment to live for the present because tomorrow might not come.

Losing my biological father taught me to embrace a loving relationship with my stepfather. The unconditional love of two dads in my life was truly a gift. I could have stayed stuck in the negative, but instead I was learning how to take my life back, even at that age.

When dealing with such significant life events, I think it is important to remember that it is natural and perfectly acceptable to take a period of time to grieve and be sad, but we mustn't get stuck there. We need to look for the positive and choose to move forward.

Everyday life also brings challenges that might not be as traumatic as a loved one's death but are nonetheless significant and play an important role in how happy we are. At the beginning of my racing career, I experienced a problem that I hadn't seen coming. In May 2003, after months of intense training in the Queen of Diamonds jet car owned by Al and Ellen Hanna of Hanna Motorsports, I was excited to be scheduled to race in my first official competitive racing event, Jet Warz at Norwalk Raceway in Ohio. It was my first time racing at night, my first time racing against a competitor in the other lane, and my first time racing in front of spectators. I was shocked when I realized that there were thirty thousand people in attendance and was honestly a bit intimidated by it all.

I was super excited to go to my first official drivers' meeting, but that excitement quickly faded when every one of the other drivers, who happened to all be male, refused to shake my hand during introductions. Seriously? Was I being given the cold shoulder because I was the only female in the room, or was that just how they treated all the newbies? I honestly didn't care. I just didn't appreciate it.

My first reaction was to be deeply hurt, but it was clear that I had a choice to make. I could let this rejection affect my mental state so much that I stopped believing that I belonged there; I could get so rattled that I lost focus on the actual race; I could respond with anger and create all kinds of drama; or—and this is what I did—I could use that moment of disrespect and rejection to create my own R.U.S.H. opportunity. I ignored their poor behavior, reaffirmed my belief in myself and my right to be there, and focused on being the best driver out there. I won the entire event that night and received the title of Jet Warz World Champion. I went on to continually kick those same drivers' butts on the track for my entire five-year racing career as "Jessie Harris—Queen of Diamonds."

The fact of the matter is that even if I hadn't won the event that night, I still would have felt victorious because I intentionally did not accept that feeling of rejection and I made the choices that were best for me. I looked for that R.U.S.H. opportunity and created a more positive focus. It's nice to be able to say that those drivers and I became friends over the years, but I know that happened only because of the choices I made at that first drivers' meeting.

Queen of Diamonds Jet Dragster; Jessie Harris Bouton; Jet Warz Trophy, 2003

I think it is important to stress to you right up front that using the power of intentional living can make your life so much better, but it is in no way a magic wand that can make all things wrong in our world right again. It cannot guarantee that bad things will never happen. There are always some life-altering events that take place. When they hit you and knock you to your knees, you say to yourself, "I will never be happy again," and through your tears, you know it to be true. And you'll be right, in a sense. You will never view the world the same way again, never experience happiness the same way again, and never be the same person you once were. Your life will have been permanently altered.

Knowing this, I want you to hold fast to a truth about intentional living. No matter what happens in our lives—even when things happen that make us know in the depths of our souls that we will never be the same again (a divorce, a death, abuse, a major loss of any type)—we can find happiness again. Perhaps it will be different from the way we have known it in the past, but we can still create lives that allow us to move forward and be happy again.

It isn't easy, though. It isn't even necessarily something that you can do alone. Reach out to those in your life who can support you and help you grow through whatever life event has made you struggle. Don't just *live* through it, but *grow* through it also. Surround yourself with like-minded people who understand the need to respond to life events with courage and the power to live fully—never forgetting your past, always heading toward the future, but firmly and fully established in the present. Your present is truly the only reality that exists.

Sometimes moving forward may consist simply of getting out of bed in the morning and getting dressed. There are times when life deals us a hand that is truly that tough to handle, but we must not allow ourselves to get stuck there. It is essential to continue to move forward every single day, one step at a time. Even a tiny step is a step forward and is progress. Look for and find the R.U.S.H. opp. It is a deliberate choice that you alone must make. Create your own R.U.S.H. Revolution!

R.U.S.H. REVIEW-Chapter 1: The R.U.S.H. Revolution

<u>Chapter Highlights to Remember:</u>

1. Don't accept the status quo. Don't live your life on automatic. Don't accept unhappiness. Live your life with intention. Live your life on purpose.
2. Life events do not control or dictate how happy we are. We do.
3. View your problems (situations) as R.U.S.H. opps. Use your opportunities to create the life that you want.
4. Look for the positive and choose to move forward. Even a small step forward is a step in the right direction.

<u>Start your own revolution! Ask yourself these questions to begin R.U.S.H.ing:</u>

1. At the end of the day, do I feel that I lived that day for myself? Or did I live it more for others?
2. When faced with a situation that I don't like, do I take specific action to turn it into an opportunity?
3. What did I do today to keep myself moving forward?

My R.U.S.H. vision for tomorrow:

I will

_____

_____

He opened the door and helped her into the car.
"Where are we going?" she asked.
"That depends on which route you take," he
said as he handed her the keys.

Two

Infinity Factor #1: Power—Recognize that the Power Is in *You*

If you want to make any changes in your life, the first thing you must understand is that the power to make that change is in you. Successful change can never be made for someone else or because of someone else. It is always made for you and because of you. Intentional living is dependent on the awareness and acceptance of the power that is within you.

As trite as it may sound, you really are the captain of your own ship. You can chart your life course. Does that mean you won't encounter some bad weather and rough waters? No. But it means that in many instances you can adjust your sails to avoid that area; you can have emergency plans and supplies in place, and sometimes you can simply decide that you shouldn't take the boat out that particular day.

In my case, I was a professional race car driver for seven years. When I graduated from high school, I didn't have a plan for my life. I didn't like college. I was working at a job that I liked but didn't love. I wanted more. I wanted excitement, and I wanted each day of my life to feel like it mattered.

At the age of nineteen, when presented with my first R.U.S.H. opportunity, I made a conscious decision to go after a job driving a 300-mph jet car. Had I ever driven a 300-mph race car before? No. Had I ever driven a 200-mph race car before? No. I had only driven my 1995 Chevy Monte Carlo at the top speed of 84 mph down the quarter-mile drag strip. Did I have doubts? Yes. Was I nervous? Of course. I realized, though, that if I wanted a different life, I had to be willing to work for it and go after it. So I did.

This R.U.S.H. opportunity presented itself when I wasn't even prepared for it. I didn't see it coming. Although I had been involved in drag racing with my dad for years and was in the process of building my own race car, I had never had thoughts of racing professionally and certainly not of racing a jet-powered 300 -mph vehicle.

Just like most people, I thought that something like that was beyond my reach, so I had never set that as a goal. But I just happened to be in the right place at the right time, and when I was asked whether I would be interested in interviewing to drive a jet car at racetracks all across the country, instead of backing away and immediately falling victim to the "I'm not good enough, and I've never done this before" mentality, I seized the opportunity. I swear I heard an angel choir and knew this was what most call an aha moment. I puffed myself up and said, "I am absolutely interested! Where do I send my résumé, and whom should I talk to?"

A few months after sending my résumé, I received a phone call inviting me to go to Connecticut for an interview. I interviewed, trained, and landed the job driving that 300-mph jet car all around the country. That was the first time I realized that I had the power within me to change my life to anything I wanted it to be. I grabbed those car keys of life and chose the route that I wanted to take, and it was a different route than the one I'd been driving for nineteen years.

Using that power within you sometimes requires a lot of work and commitment to follow through on things, but in the end, when you create your life instead of just exist in your life, it is the most satisfying bit of awesomeness ever!

Look for opportunities. Create opportunities. Always be open to a previously unknown opportunity, and stay positive and ready to do whatever it takes to reach a new goal. Taking an active role in your life and living intentionally will always bring you greater happiness.

A passive lifestyle will allow you only to experience what others feel is best for you. Sometimes that works, and sometimes it doesn't. If you want to improve the quality of your life, you must own the responsibility for steering the boat—or the race car!

Does this scare you a little bit? Have you always had someone else making most of the decisions in your life? Has life continued to just happen, to the point that suddenly your days have gone by filled with the stress of just trying to keep up, and you feel like you didn't get anything done?

Maybe you feel that there isn't time for you anymore and that no one really knows who you are because you are so busy functioning as a parent, a spouse, a child, or an employee. You don't have time to make better meals or do something for yourself. You don't even have time to take a shower by yourself! That's OK. It is understandable to be a little bit nervous about taking a different, more proactive approach to life. That might even be the reason you're reading this book.

We are all born with the power inside of us to make choices. The idea behind intentional living is learning to see that we have choices to make; we don't have to just accept whatever each day brings. We don't have to be victims of circumstance. Each of us can make the choice to claim his or her Best Life Ever. So here's a summary:

- *Understand* that you have choices to make.
- *Accept* that you have choices to make.
- *Use* those choices to create the life that you desire most, the one that you deserve.

Don't just make the choices that other people tell you to make. Dig deep and make choices that resonate with you. Revolutionize how you think. Get ready to R.U.S.H. with flying colors!

Making a conscious choice to change your life is the first step. Believing in yourself enough to be able to make that choice is significant, but as you have always known, nothing comes for free. It is important to understand that there is a definite difference between belief in yourself and wishful thinking. What do I mean by that? I mean that it's easy to have a dream; it's easy to *say* that you want things to change and that you want to claim your Best Life Ever, but the fact of the matter is that you must take action in order to bring those dreams to fruition. You must set goals and develop action plans, or all you will have is wishful thinking.

All too often, either we don't formalize the actions of setting goals and developing action plans or—even worse—we limit our success by believing that our worst traits are eternal anchors around our necks. We believe there are things about ourselves that are weaknesses, and that affects the way we think. It drags us down and limits our vision, making us feel powerless.

The truth of the matter is that we *do* have the power, in six easy steps, to change our limiting beliefs. I know how effective this process is because I used it myself to overcome my own limiting belief that I would always be a procrastinator. Here are the steps:

Step 1—Identify a limiting belief about yourself.
Step 2—Identify the behavior that this limiting belief causes.
Step 3—Determine how that makes you feel.
Step 4—Decide how you would rather feel.
Step 5—Determine what behavior is required to achieve that, and put it into action.
Step 6 (the magic transformation step)—Recognize the new, empowering belief you have about yourself.

Using these R.U.S.H. Belief Transformation steps can help you learn how to change any limiting belief into an empowering one. You have the power to do that. Here is how I used this process regarding my own limiting belief that I would always be a procrastinator.

Step 1—A limiting belief about myself is that I am a procrastinator.
Step 2—Some behaviors associated with that belief include not completing tasks; feeling scattered, stressed, and impatient; overcommitting; not being able to sleep; eating poorly; feeling less connected with family; and making excuses.
Step 3—The result of that behavior is that I feel awful. I blame others, have self-doubt, self-sabotage, feel like a failure, don't feel loving, feel disconnected, feel less desirable, and experience emotional pain and fear.

Step 4—How would I rather feel? I want to feel successful, happy, centered, effective, loving, loved, self-aware, desired, invincible, accomplished, connected to people, congruent, grounded, and confident.

Step 5—Which behaviors will make me feel that way? I will commit to things I want to do, schedule things on my calendar, follow through, stop creating excuses, use positive affirmations and empowering statements, take better care of myself, create solid boundaries (say no, guard my time), perform high-level actions and delegate what I can, and visualize and stay focused on desired results.

Step 6—My new, empowering belief is that I am worthy, strong, committed, fearless, and the queen of my time (management). My new behaviors and actions make me proactive in my life and no longer a procrastinator.

Having a vision and a plan are integral parts of any successful endeavor. It doesn't matter what the end goal is. Visualizing and planning are the only ways it can be achieved successfully. There is power in this! As a professional race car driver, I learned about this in a whole new way.

You see, all race car drivers are not the same, but all race car drivers must do one thing that is the same in order to run and win their race. They need to climb into the driver's seat. That may sound simplistic, but the truth is that getting in that driver's seat suddenly makes you see things a bit differently. Suddenly you realize that the vehicle isn't going to move unless you put it in motion. You realize that you had better know the vehicle well, or you will not be able to use it to its maximum potential. You realize that you need to maintain the vehicle, or it won't run at all. And you realize that whether it goes straight down the track to the final destination or takes side trips off the beaten path, it is because you as the driver are responsible for steering.

You need to keep your eye on (visualize) the finish line in order to stay on course, and you need to have a plan. Once you understand the significance of being in the driver's seat, you then need to learn that specific car's driving sequence; you may have to rev up the motor, prime the clutch, or shift gears to allow for peak performance. Every vehicle is different. You can't just step on the gas for the entire drive, and you can't just ease down the track at a speed that can't win. You must be mindful of the vehicle's needs and act accordingly. With that said, you also need to expect the unexpected. Things happen that we never see coming, and it's important to be prepared to react on a moment's notice.

I say all this not because I think you are likely to become a race car driver but because the need for visualizing and planning applies to our everyday lives as well. We are responsible for driving our own lives in the direction that we want them to go. By knowing ourselves well—what fuels and motivates us and where we want to go—we can learn to set realistic goals, develop action plans, and use that power to achieve success.

Setting a goal is important. Dream a little (or a lot). Think about what you really want your life to be about. What would make your life happier? Set your goal, and then write it down. Pin it up somewhere where you can see it. Soak it in. Know in your heart and brand into your brain that your goal is exactly where you want to be in your life. On days when you are not so sure about things, look at that goal again and think about it. You wrote it down. You want this.

Next, take that goal and break it down so it is not quite so intimidating. Develop an action plan that sets out more manageable pieces as subgoals. That will keep you taking action one step at a time, which will eventually lead you to that lofty primary goal. Remind yourself that all things take time, energy, and effort. It can't happen overnight, remember? There is no magic wand. It takes work and action, but it can be done. A structure is built one piece at a time. A game is won one score at a time. A song is sung one note at a time. In the end, the result is almost always worth it.

The main point to remember here is simple. Only *you* can make changes in your life and make it what you want it to be. Visualize what you want, and create your plan. You need to own your life and make it happen. You can!

Infinity Factor #1: Recognize that the power is in y*ou*.

R.U.S.H. REVIEW-Chapter 2: Power

Chapter Highlights to Remember:

1. You alone have the power to make successful life changes to create the life you desire most.
2. Drive the car! Know where you want to go, and watch for and create the way to claim your Best Life Ever.
3. Develop action plans and implement them. Ideas without actions are only dreams.

Start your own revolution! Ask yourself these questions to begin R.U.S.H.ing:

1. Do I really feel that I have the power to make my life what I want it to be, or do I believe that my life is based more on what others in my life want it to be? Do I say "I can't" a lot?
2. If I could have whatever I wanted in my life, what would I have? If I could be whatever I wanted to be, what would I be?
3. I say that I want to be more successful, or I want to have more money, but what actions do I take to help me achieve those goals?

My R.U.S.H. vision for tomorrow:

I will

_____

_____

"It's so hard to sit on this stool," she said. "It isn't steady."
Carefully, he added a third leg to the stool—perfect balance.

Three

INFINITY FACTOR #2: PHILOSOPHY—
ADOPT A 3-D APPROACH TO WELLNESS

Creating a positive and productive lifestyle requires an approach to life that is whole and complete. It requires a philosophy that allows each major dimension of our lives to be explored and intentionally nurtured using a total wellness concept—a 3-D approach. The dimensions that I am referring to are body, mind, and soul. To achieve total wellness and the best quality of life, we must intentionally and consistently feed each of these areas. Doing so will create a healthy life balance.

• • •

The first dimension to consider is the *body*. To keep our bodies healthy and fit, we must fuel them and use them properly. It doesn't matter what age we are or what health issues we have; we always have the ability to eat cleanly and healthily, and there is always an exercise program that can accommodate any type of physical health issue.

We don't put diesel fuel in a gas engine and expect it to perform at peak level, so why would we expect our bodies to operate well when we eat junk food and foods high in preservatives every day? Learn about good nutrition and superfoods to achieve the healthiest body possible. You might be surprised how certain foods can help reduce blood pressure and cholesterol, improve the immune system, increase iron, reduce bloating, increase energy, and serve many other functions that help you feel better and be well.

Planning a meal schedule that allows healthy choices is not only smart but also something that's easy to implement if you commit to using the power within you to actually do it. The key to serving healthier meals is simply to commit to seeking out and choosing healthy recipes for the entire week and doing your grocery shopping based on that menu plan. Does that take a little extra work? Maybe, but that extra time spent planning is well worth it to keep you on track for a whole week of better choices.

Does committing to a healthier eating plan mean that you can never have sweets or junk food, like pizza? No! I detest dieting. Diets never work for me because I eventually stop following them. I have found that the way to stick with healthier eating is to make it a lifestyle change.

I was so used to eating larger portions that I didn't even realize how many calories I was consuming at each sitting. I pretty much ate what I wanted whenever I wanted, and then I wondered why I had gained weight. When I was racing, I was often so busy I ate only one large meal a day: brownies and Powerade. When I became a mom, I found that I would eat all day, and it would be whatever was quick to grab, which was usually processed food. Neither of these habits were healthy or smart.

As part of my personal R.U.S.H. Revolution, I made a conscious choice to make a change. I reduced my portions by one-third, and 80 percent of the time I ate foods that were healthier options. The other 20 percent of the time I splurged and had that piece of birthday cake or glass of wine. I learned to intentionally eat five small meals a day, including healthy snacks, and I also increased my water intake to half my body weight in ounces per day. It didn't take long for me to feel a difference both physically and mentally. My body felt better and looked better, and I had far less guilt regarding what I ate. Score!

Another way to take care of our bodies is to exercise. We don't expect our cars to run well if we don't do maintenance on them—changing the oil, rotating the tires, and changing the air filter. Why do we expect our bodies to feel good and perform well if we don't exercise regularly, build and maintain muscle, and eliminate fat?

Using the power within, I changed my course and set a plan to start incorporating some sort of exercise into my daily routine. Sometimes I followed a particular workout program; other times I took walks around my neighborhood with my kids and my dog. Playing with my children actually became a great choice for getting exercise because it netted me three things: I got my exercise for the day, I got to spend quality time with my kids, and I instilled good habits in them (which is probably the best thing). Everybody won.

As a bonus, physical exercise has been determined to do something that a lot of people don't even realize. When you exercise, your body releases chemicals called endorphins, which trigger a positive physical feeling. Exercise also helps to reduce stress, reverses the effects of aging, increases memory retention, and increases heart health. Lastly, it is a sure way to help you look and feel better about yourself.

The last thing to remember about taking care of our bodies has to do with staying current with our annual doctors' appointments. Many times, even with nutritious food and regular exercise, our bodies need some additional help to keep us at our healthiest levels. Annual examinations can identify any chemical imbalances or medical disorders that need to be monitored and medicated to keep us well. Needing medication should not be viewed as a weakness. Identification of specific issues at an early stage and the initiation of a proper treatment plan can add so much quality to our lives, which can be viewed only as a strength.

• • •

The second dimension to discuss in the 3-D total wellness concept is the *mind*. Some say each of us is blessed with whatever mind we each have and that's that, but that's not really the whole story. Yes, each of us is blessed with a beautiful, unique mind, but just like anything else, what you put into it can definitely affect what comes out of it.

Our minds basically make computations based on whatever data has been entered into our brains. They don't add in whether what we have fed them is true or false, right or wrong, or even complete. They use whatever data has been stored away in our minds and determine a course of action based on that. Consequently, it is very important that we continually feed our minds with facts and knowledge and not just incomplete or biased opinions.

To keep our minds physically healthy, it is important to eat well by choosing good, nutritious foods. Don't forget to check the superfood list. There are many specific foods that can boost your brain power and reduce the risk of dementia. Some examples would be foods rich in omega-3 fatty acids (flax and chia seeds, salmon, and sardines), olive oil, walnuts, beets, berries, and spinach. Do your research. There are many other superfoods that contain high levels of much-needed vitamins and minerals.

Get ample rest. The National Sleep Foundation recommends seven to nine hours of sleep for adults.

Keep your mind stimulated with mental activities. Exercising your mind is similar to exercising your body; it works better if it is used regularly.

Minds are powerful. If the mind believes something strongly enough, it can actually change not only our mental states but also our physical reactions to things. It doesn't necessarily matter whether a belief is true or not. It only matters whether our minds believe it to be true. For example, if you hear a noise in the middle of the night, you might believe one of two things. If you think it's just a branch in the wind, you will roll over and go back to sleep. If you immediately assume it to be someone trying to break into your house, however, fear will cause a physical reaction. Your mouth will get dry and you will start to sweat as that fear envelops your total being and you go into a fight-or-flight stress response. My point here is that the truth regarding what the noise was has nothing to do with your response. Your response is based on what your mind believes.

What our minds believe is immensely powerful. As our parents tried to teach us when we were young, the people we surround ourselves with and what we do each day can have a tremendous impact on our lives. Everything we put into our minds becomes who we are. People we spend time with, books we read, movies we watch, activities we choose, knowledge we gain through continued education—all of these become part of who we are. It is important to choose wisely what we feed our minds.

• • •

The third dimension of total wellness has to do with feeding your *soul.* I believe that our souls are the nonphysical parts of us that embody our moral and emotional natures. The soul allows for the ability to feel kindness and sympathy and to appreciate beauty, art, and music. Many people, including me, believe that the soul is eternal and will continue to exist after the physical body dies.

Although opinions may vary, I am certain that feeding the soul and ministering to the soul in some way is an essential part of our 3-D wellness concept. Our bodies and minds gather and process information. Our minds follow directions and think and reason using the information they are aware of, but they cannot exist without our bodies. The body and mind are partners. But our souls tell us how we feel about things. And how we feel has a direct effect on what choices we make in our lives.

Generally speaking, if something makes us feel good, we will do it, and if something doesn't make us feel good, we will not do it. This starts to become a little bit complex when what makes us feel good in the present eventually makes us not feel good in the future. Once we recognize this, though, we can start through intentional living to make better decisions that will allow us to feel good in both the present and the future. Our souls house our emotions and are capable of moral judgment. The soul creates our nonphysical sense of well-being. Feeding our souls will allow us to find our happiest state in life.

The answer to how to feed your soul is different for everyone, but in general, you should feed your soul with something that causes you to feel a sense of purpose and fulfillment, something that creates a harmony and peaceful balance in your life and often a feeling of being part of something greater than yourself. You will need to determine what works best for you. Some examples of activities that may feed your soul are spending time listening to music that stirs your emotions, reading books that lift you up and allow you to grow, attending church services, supporting volunteer activities, or practicing yoga.

Spending quality time with my family and helping others are things that allow me to feed my soul. Whether I am playing games with my family or having family dinners; volunteering my time, money, or services at local shelters or food kitchens; or bringing food to a friend, elderly neighbor, or new parents, I feel proud and happy to have done a selfless thing. Maybe working at an animal shelter is what feeds your soul, or maybe it's creating artwork or meditating. It can be many different things, but feeding that non-physical part of you can create a positive aura around you. Do it!

• • •

The bottom line for this infinity factor is that you should embrace each of the dimensions of total wellness with the understanding that if one dimension is not attended to, there will be a negative effect. It is a bit like trying to sit on a three-legged stool. If one of the legs is missing, you will probably not be able to sit very comfortably.

Infinity Factor #2: Adopt a 3-D approach to wellness philosophy. Nurture your body, mind, and soul.

R.U.S.H. REVIEW-Chapter 3: Philosophy

Chapter Highlights to Remember:

1. Body—eat right and exercise regularly.
2. Mind—stimulate your mind. Feed it with care.
3. Soul—find and do things that bring you a sense of purpose and fulfillment.

Start your own revolution! Ask yourself these questions to begin R.U.S.H.ing:

1. Do I plan healthy meals and snacks for myself and my family? What type of exercise do I get every day?
2. How do I feed my mind every day? Do I read or learn new things? What things do I do that require me to use critical thinking skills or sharpen my cognitive functions?
3. What do I do in my life that allows me to feel fulfilled? What do I do to enrich my spiritual well-being?

My R.U.S.H. vision for tomorrow:

I will

_____

_____

"Although beautiful, my life is not what I
want it to be," she told him.
"Then you must choose a new direction," he said.

Four

INFINITY FACTOR #3: PURPOSE—MAKE
DELIBERATE CHOICES AND DECISIONS

The very heart of intentional living revolves around having a purpose, knowing your purpose, and making choices and decisions that support your purpose. The first tricky part about purpose is determining exactly what your purpose in life is and actually putting a name to it. Then you must write it out in the form of a personal mission statement so that you can see it and reflect on it daily. The second tricky part about purpose is understanding that it needs to be practiced every day for you to benefit from it as part of your intentional lifestyle.

Determining a life purpose is very personal and is different for different people. It is all about what gives meaning to your life—what makes you feel fulfilled and thus leads to a higher level of self-happiness. Your purpose reflects what you decide you want your life to communicate to others and what you want to contribute to the world.

This can be such a hard assignment for the average person, mainly because few have ever really thought about it before. It takes time and effort to truly reflect on your inner self, examining strengths, weaknesses, values, and beliefs. But knowing this key information about yourself will pave the way for you to make deliberate choices and decisions in your life that can and will improve your self-happiness. A sense of purpose produces positive physical, psychological, and spiritual benefits as well. Science has linked having a sense of purpose to a reduction in physical ailments and depression and to an increase in a sense of fulfillment and self-happiness.

The biggest thing that naming your life purpose brings to you is a defined way to make choices and decisions that you feel certain of and can benefit from. Too often, we are told that we need to make good choices, but we don't feel quite sure of how to do that. Determining what your life purpose is, writing it out as a personal mission statement, and then making choices and decisions that align with it *is* the "how" when it comes to revving up self-happiness.

Creating a personal mission statement to live by is a product of self-discovery. It is a statement that you develop to provide clarity in your life based on your natural and developed talents and skills, your values and priorities, and your desires for your future. It helps you to align all the choices and decisions you make with your highest life priorities. It allows you to make those hard choices using sound knowledge about yourself instead of leaving them to chance or making choices because someone else thinks they're right.

It can be one sentence or one hundred sentences, but the objective of the statement is to use what you learn about yourself and write down what you want to commit your life to. It is a written-down purpose for your life that you can hang on your wall or refrigerator door so that you see it often. When you see it, you can remind yourself of the type of deliberate actions you should be taking to move yourself forward.

If you are uncertain about how to develop a mission or purpose statement for your life on your own, research it online, sign up for a class, or enlist the help of a mentor. It is that important! In my online business courses (at infinitywellnessproject.com), students are led through the process of developing their own mission or purpose statement (R.U.S.H. Plan), and they often tell me how excited they are to learn how to do this in more detail, because it is truly empowering. It is empowering because it provides students with their own personal road maps so that they can make the choices that are right for them, choices they can be confident about.

My own personal purpose statement has evolved over time. I started out with a statement that was fairly short and broad: to grow and to give. I have found, however, that I am better suited to one that is more detailed. Mine is now two pages long and includes the following sections:

Section 1: Who I Am and Who I Want to Be
Section 2: My Priorities in Life
Section 3: My Professional Realm
Section 4: My Personal Realm
Section 5: My Legacy
Section 6: Intentional Life Management

A purpose statement may take time and energy to develop, but it can be the single most important thing you do when it comes to living your life intentionally and achieving your most fulfilling life. It is your personal guide to making the best decisions and choices for your life.

We always have choices, but sometimes we don't feel like we do. It is very easy to get sucked into the Big Guilt Vacuum. And if we escape from that, too often we find ourselves drifting through our lives with absolutely no thought as to why we are doing the things we do; we're just going through the motions, cruising along on automatic, and doing whatever ends up in front of us. We live our lives with no clear intention or destination in mind, and, as a result, we eventually start to feel unhappy and out of control. If that is the case, it needs to change. Rev up your self-happiness. R.U.S.H.! Take your life back!

As far as I'm concerned, learning to find happiness should be included in the basic lesson plan of every kindergarten class and continue straight through to every college-course syllabus. They teach other things in school that are necessary to live life well: how to feed your body, take care of your body, spell words, speak clearly, add numbers, read a book, dissect a frog, write a resume, and get passing grades. They teach you who discovered America and who invented electricity and who was president in 1963, but they don't seem to teach you much about how to learn who you really are or how to live life on purpose instead of in reaction mode. They don't teach you that you have the power to be exactly who you want to be or how to go about becoming that person.

You are the discoverer and inventor of *you*. You have the power to be and the power to do whatever makes you happiest in life. So how do you do that? You do that by living your life intentionally—on purpose, by making deliberate choices and decisions, and by setting goals.

It's important to focus on your goals, your win light—whatever it is that you really want—so you can know what direction to go in and what choices to make. Your win light should actually be a goal that you have set that aligns with your life purpose. Focusing on your win light is what I call getting into the R.U.S.H. zone. When making choices and decisions, use my win-light process by focusing and asking yourself two things:

1. Why am I doing this?
2. Does this enhance or add value to my life?

When you ask yourself why you are taking this action, take some time to think about it. Is the reason you are doing something one that will lead you closer to your win light (your goal)? Once you know why you are doing something, you can then determine whether it really adds value to your life. Every intentional thing you do should add value to your life in some way. If it doesn't, my guess is you are doing it for the wrong reasons, which will eventually lead to unhappiness.

The benefit of using this win-light process is that you will feel more content with your life and the decisions you make. This can lessen stress and bring a happier tone to your life. You won't feel so out of control and overwhelmed. A big advantage of this is that you will find yourself starting to become more aware that you really do have a choice about everything you do in your life. Every single thing.

Let me use my own life as an example. Back in my race car driving days I was pretty good at focusing on my win light, even though it changed as time went on. When I applied for the position, I just wanted to drive. Once I was hired as a driver, I found that I didn't just want to drive. I wanted to race and win. To win, everything had to be just right. I needed to be in the R.U.S.H. zone. The car had to be in top condition, the track needed to be well prepared, and I needed to be fully suited up in safety gear and have my mind in the right place. I needed to focus on the start-up sequence of the jet engine and then completely close myself off from all distractions. I needed to focus on the race and the driving skills needed to win it. I couldn't be worried about what people around me were doing or what they were thinking. I couldn't think about whether my competitor had more skills or a better car. I had to run my own race and be confident in myself. I had to be totally focused on what I wanted and fearless about going after it.

In five years I lost only one race, and I lost that race because I lost my focus. My opponent and I had a fierce rivalry, and he was notorious for playing games on the starting line. Instead of focusing on my mission and running my own race, I allowed the competition to get into my head. That distraction caused me to not fully account for the track conditions and how my vehicle would be affected.

I lost only one out of approximately six hundred races, setting a record as the winningest jet car driver in history. I attribute my record of success to having a competitive race car and an excellent race team and to using this mental win-light process.

When I asked myself why I wanted to race and win, I found that I wanted the success not only for myself and my team but also for my fans—the people I was a role model for—to show them that anyone can achieve their dreams. This added value to my life because it related back to my life purpose, which was about continual personal growth and inspiring and helping others.

My racing career also added value to my life in a variety of ways that were unexpected. It taught me not only how to race a car and develop skills to win but also how to become more independent in my life, become a better public speaker, motivate and inspire others, develop a platform for organ donation, and improve my communication skills.

Interacting with fans and being a role model for others was extremely gratifying. This part of my life was a dream come true, and I found that as much as I enjoyed racing the car, it was in interacting with fans and inspiring people that I had found my true passion.

As time went on, I found that my win light had changed based on my life experiences. At the end of my five-year racing contract I needed to make a significant decision: whether to extend my contract driving the jet car and continue that wildly successful journey or to step away from the jet car and pursue a new direction that might better align with my new goal.

Many people felt it would be foolish to abandon a known good thing, and, at times, so did I. By getting into the R.U.S.H. zone and focusing on the two questions in my win-light process, I was able to make a decision with confidence, one that was not based on emotion.

I knew in my heart that what I wanted—personal growth, a better salary, and to become a driver for a Top Fuel racing team (the highest category in the sport)—was in direct alignment with what brought meaning to my life. The increased media coverage would be an excellent way for me to continue to inspire others as well as to increase public awareness for my primary platform, organ donation.

The Top Fuel Drag Racing sport was political to some degree and cost upward of $3 million a year, making driving positions few in number and highly competitive. Twice I landed a driving position but was heartbroken when neither one materialized. I lost the first position due to the US economic decline, which caused our corporate sponsor backing to fall through. I lost the second due to team owners who reneged on their agreement with me and cut a deal with a different driver who brought more money to the table.

It was a very difficult time for me. What I want you to know, though, is that my decision to walk away from the jet car and toward the Top Fuel industry was not a bad one. It was the right one for me at the time, and while my Top Fuel dream did not materialize, I found much joy in the time I spent pursuing it and the contacts that I made along the way. Continual use of my win-light process (asking why and what the value is) helped me to know which choices to make and to feel confident in making them. I do not regret a thing, and that is winning.

When I got married and started a family, I was happy and excited to have another of my dreams come true. I was focused and fearless and totally in control; I just wasn't racing a jet car anymore. But then life started moving at a very fast pace, and it was no longer all about me. All my choices and decisions had a direct impact on my husband and little boys.

I had so many responsibilities, from being a mom and wife to doing some work from home for our family-owned physical therapy clinic, that they started to take over my life. I started to lose my own identity. Gone was the "cool," race car driving, independent woman who spoke at national events and inspired and motivated people every day by using her career as a platform to raise awareness for organ donation. I didn't feel cool. I didn't feel in control of my life, and I started feeling depressed and unappreciated. I felt as though I didn't really matter. I felt loved and needed, of course, but not in the way that I was accustomed to and not in the way that provided me with a sense of total value.

My purpose and my passion in life—helping others to realize that they could reach their dreams—was missing. I had stopped "feeding" that part of my life in order to take care of my family, and as rewarding as raising a family could be, it wasn't enough for me to feel fulfilled. The fact that I was just going through the motions of living every day only made things worse. Feeling unfulfilled and depressed was my motivator to make changes in my life. How I felt every day wasn't pleasant. I was in pain. For a while I thought that this was just my destiny, that I had chosen marriage and a family and had therefore sacrificed some of my own needs and desires.

This was not the truth at all, but my mind had convinced me that it was. It was in this pain that I suddenly realized that if I wanted to change how I felt, I needed to do something different. If I wanted to see things differently, I had to change where I was standing and move to the other side of the street. Because I was so unhappy, I felt desperate enough to rebel against what life had handed me and to try to take back some control.

So I made a *choice* to stop blaming my life and the events in it for my depression and to start owning my life again. I *chose* to make a change, to take control and live my life with purpose—to live by choice and not by chance. I began using my win-light process for everything in my life. I focused on what I wanted my win light to be, and for every task I needed to do, every choice and decision I had to make, I asked myself, "Why am I doing this?" Then I asked, "Does this enhance my life? Does it add value?" I was amazed that I had forgotten how certain things added value to my life and how others simply didn't add value at all. I became very deliberate and intentional about every single thing I did during my day, and my R.U.S.H. mantra became, "If it doesn't enhance, I left it to chance!"

For example, as much as I hate certain household chores, I make a conscious decision to do them because of the value added for me and my entire family. But I have also made decisions that, when I got into the zone and gave them the win-light test, did not enhance my life. In fact, they added stress to my life instead. For instance, I agreed to be the fund-raising chairperson for my child's class when I really didn't want to; somehow I got sucked into the Big Guilt Vacuum when that decision was made. And there were times when I did things with or for family members that I really didn't want to do and didn't have time for.

At the time, I felt like I didn't have a choice, like I had to do those things because family adds value to my life. But that is not always true. Sometimes doing those things will add value to their lives but create stress and resentment in yours. Although it may not be an easy decision to say no, sometimes it is the right decision for you. Saying no can often open a new path via compromise that can add value to your life and to others' lives.

I need to stress, however, that although I am a strong advocate of making deliberate choices that add value and contribute to your overall happiness, I never intend for those choices to be used as excuses to be unkind. What I mean is that it is not OK to be selfish and hurt others. Sometimes the value in doing something is in making someone else happy. There are times in all our lives when something means more to someone else than it does to us. If that is the case, perhaps your choice could be to grant the person that happiness. The world does not and should not revolve only around me or you.

Infinity Factor #3: Know your *purpose*; make deliberate choices and decisions.

R.U.S.H. REVIEW-Chapter 4: Purpose

Chapter Highlights to Remember:

1. Know your life purpose. Know what your priorities in life are and what gives you a sense of fulfillment.
2. Make wise choices and decisions that directly align with your life purpose.
3. Use the win-light process to stay on track; ask yourself why you are doing the things you're doing and whether they add value to your life.

Start your own revolution! Ask yourself these questions to begin R.U.S.H.ing:

1. Do I really know what my life purpose is? Have I put it into words in the form of a written personal mission statement?
2. When I make choices and decisions in my life, do I make them for the right reasons? Do they align with my highest priorities in life?
3. Have I ever asked myself why I am doing something? Have I ever realized that I spend a lot of time doing things that matter to someone else but not to me?

My R.U.S.H. vision for tomorrow:

I will

_____

_____

"I can't see!" she cried. "It's so dark that I can't find my way." She sat down and started to weep in the darkness. Gently, he took her hand and put it on the light switch. "The power is there," he said. "You just need to turn it on."

Five

There have been many studies done on the power of positive thinking, and I have always been intrigued by the results. Some things can be explained scientifically, and some things have not been explained scientifically but still seem to exist. I believe it's perfectly OK if we don't understand why something happens as long as we recognize that it *does* happen and that we can use it for good.

Have you ever heard of the idea that whatever you look for, you will find? I believe that thought is absolutely grounded in truth. If you look for a red car, you usually end up seeing one. If you look for a bad habit in someone, you'll probably find one. If you look for a smile, you'll find someone who offers one, and if you look for a frown, you'll find that too. This idea is extremely powerful. It's a way we can use the control we have in our lives to focus on things that are positive and not negative—things that lift us up and don't drag us down. Try it. I assure you that it really works! And if I can give you a tip: look for the right things in life, things that make you happy. Look for the goodness in life, because it is there.

Has anyone ever told you that you weren't good enough or deserving of whatever you dreamed about? If so, did you stop to determine why that person said those things? Was it because they were true? Or was it because the person didn't want to see you succeed because it didn't benefit him or her in some way? This type of thing happens to people all the time, so it's important that we remember to focus on what we want in our lives. What we look for, we find.

When I was making my decision to leave the jet car world and pursue my new racing direction, I experienced some negativity and attacks on my character. I began to expect to hear these types of comments daily and almost started to believe them. It brought me to tears many times. Was I really not deserving or capable of reaching for my dream? Had I not been appreciative enough of the jet car racing career I had enjoyed so much?

No, I was deserving and appreciative. Moving in a new direction was not selfish. I needed to take myself out of the negative and intentionally seek out the positive. There were many people in my professional life who acknowledged my skill and desire to move forward and offered assistance in helping me do that. I will always be grateful to them.

While dealing with all that in my professional life, I was also feeling stressed in my personal life. My boyfriend (now-husband), Chris, had been on the national kidney transplant list for two years without a donor match. Why was Chris so sick? He didn't deserve that. Finally, Chris's brother had improved and maintained his own health enough that he was approved to donate one of his kidneys. But the prospect of surgery was frightening. Fortunately, Chris and his brother came through the surgery just fine and are healthy today. At the time, though, my personal life was just as stressful as my professional life.

Life didn't seem so good on the inside, even though outsiders thought I had it all. To keep a long story short, I needed to look for the goodness in life to feel better. If I had focused on just the negative, I would have quit, shut down on my life, but I looked for the goodness and the good people, and that's what kept my life centered. Again, what you look for, you will find.

Take firm control over how you spend your time and who you spend it with. Doing these things alone will help you to feel calmer and more content with your life overall.

Some people are chronic complainers. That's just what they do—they complain all the time and never seem happy. If you spend a lot of time around that type of person, more than likely you will end up the same way. You will feel sad and depressed. You will not have energy and will just generally feel unhappy. Conversely, if you spend time around people who count their blessings and look for the silver lining, you will feel much happier and more energized. You will smile and laugh more. Remember what so many of our mamas told us growing up (we all heard it at one time or another): "You are who you surround yourself with."

Also be mindful of how you spend your time. If you spend hours of time watching violent, bloody movies, reading gory suspense novels, or focusing on tragic headlines in the news, your world will be tainted with darkness and negative vibes.

To have a positive life, you must do things that lend themselves to that end. Remember, to rev up your self-happiness, you need to first know what you want and then take actions to get there. Be careful of spending too much time surrounded by people who think that happiness comes as a gift and that they have no control over it. Those people will not be helpful in your quest for a happier, more fulfilling life. Don't allow anyone to take that away from you. You have a choice. If certain people don't enhance your life, don't spend time with them. Gently find ways to let them go from your life, or at least minimize the time spent with them. Surround yourself with positive people. Find yourself a R.U.S.H. buddy.

R.U.S.H. buddies can save your life at times. Trust me, I know this. A R.U.S.H. buddy can be defined as someone who has your best interests at heart, who supports you through thick and thin, and who is there to hold you accountable for your actions (or lack thereof). R.U.S.H. buddies know when you can't find the silver lining in that black cloud that's been hanging over you, and they reach right up and pull it down to form a crown on your head. R.U.S.H. buddies know when you can't stand on your own, so they put their arms under your shoulders for support. They know that there are times when only tears can wash away the pain, and they hand you tissues to dry your cheeks. They don't always ask questions and they don't always have answers, but they have love for you and a smile, and they always try to bring happiness into your life. R.U.S.H. buddies bring positive light to you and those important to you. They lift you up. Do they add value to your life? You bet they do! Strive to keep them in it.

One of my most influential and appreciated R.U.S.H. buddies was also one of my mentors. Mr. Frank Hawley is a legend in the sport of drag racing. My relationship with him began when I was a student at his prestigious racing school (Frank Hawley Drag Racing School) in Gainesville, Florida. He later became a friend and an advocate of my pursuit for the Top Fuel Drag Racing category. This man taught me not only how to hone my natural talent behind the wheel of high-horsepower race cars but also how to develop the ability to be direct and unemotional whether I was explaining mechanical issues or dealing with the personalities and politics of the sport. I will never forget the example he set and the unselfish actions he took to help me become the best I could be. His words were direct and sometimes hard to hear, but he always had my best interests in mind. He took the best and the worst in me and helped me to become better. That's what true R.U.S.H. buddies do.

Jessie with Frank Hawley, Drag Racing Legend and Mentor

Choosing activities that bring light and happiness into your realm is also important. Too often, it seems, we don't choose wisely. Change that! Choose music that is uplifting. Choose fun activities with family and friends that don't create friction and frustration. Don't just watch movies for hours or sit in different rooms. Choose to go outside and get fresh air and do something together. Whether it's a picnic or a softball game, a play or a symphony, church or museums, car rides or helping clean up a neighbor's yard, choose activities that make you feel good.

Surrounding yourself with darkness can quickly become mood altering and depressing. If it starts getting dark, pull out a flashlight.

Change your environment and do something to let the light in. But you have to take action. It won't just happen by itself. Choose the positive, do the positive, and then repeat it over and over again.

The power of light and positivity is astounding! You don't have to understand it; just use it to bring the highest level of energy and goodness into your life.

Infinity Factor #4: Stay positive. Avoid negative people, activities, and thoughts.

R.U.S.H. REVIEW-Chapter 5: Positivity

Chapter Highlights to Remember:

1. There is power in positive thinking that is not always easily explained by science.
2. What you look for you tend to find.
3. R.U.S.H. buddies can get you through.

Start your own revolution! Ask yourself these questions to begin R.U.S.H.ing:

1. Have I ever told myself that I couldn't do something and been right? Have I ever told myself that I definitely could do something and then did, even though the odds were against me?
2. Have I ever been in a bad mood, and it seemed like everything in the day just went wrong? Do I ever have people tell me that I always see the good in people?
3. Who do I turn to for support and comfort in my life? Do I search for the people who understand and support my ambitions, or do I feel that I don't need people like that in my life?

My R.U.S.H. vision for tomorrow:

I will

"How quickly time goes by," she said. "If only I could slow it down."
"That cannot be done," he said. "You can only
eliminate the time that is wasted."

Six

INFINITY FACTOR #5: PURGE—
ELIMINATE TIME WASTERS

Have you ever gone through an entire day and realized at the end of it that you didn't get nearly as much done as you would have liked? The day started out right. You had your coffee and breakfast and had a good plan for what needed to happen, and then…it didn't happen. The day flew by, and you had little to show for it.

That's happened to me and to many others that I have known. It is not unusual, but it is a little annoying. And if it becomes a pattern that is repeated day after day, you can lose a lot of valuable time that could have been used to do something of worth—something that would have made you feel good rather than depressed. Understand that every day that goes by, every hour, every minute, every second spent, is gone, never to return. You will never get that time back. We shouldn't waste something so precious.

Part of intentional living means not only knowing who we are, who we want to become, what we prioritize in our lives, and what we want to do, but also taking actions to keep us true to our life purposes. If at the end of the day we are sitting there wondering what really happened and why we don't seem to have enough time to accomplish the things we want to do, then we need to examine the cause first and implement an action second.

I did an experiment once to see where my time was going by writing down in a little spiral notebook everything I did during my day and how much time I spent doing it. I did this for two weeks. When I reviewed my journal at the end of the two weeks, I was actually shocked by how much time I had wasted—totally wasted—without even realizing it. When I tell you I was shocked, it's because if you had asked me how much time I spent on social media or watching television, there's no way I would have told you the number I had written in that journal. My mind just didn't add it up that way until I saw it in black and white.

That was a total oh-my-God moment for me. It was a true moment of clarity when I saw how quickly time wasters could take over my life and leave me in the shadows. It was evident to me that if I wanted my life to be more valuable, I needed to stop wasting time and to actively choose the way I wanted to spend my limited number of minutes. I needed to purge my life of things that did not relate to my life purpose. The next few paragraphs cover some time wasters I was guilty of and what I learned.

Unplug. Do *not* spend hours and hours on e-mail or social media. Specifically, only check e-mail during certain times of the day, maybe for one hour in the morning or one hour in the afternoon. Limit time on social media, television, the Internet, and so on. You can lose *hours* before you know it.

Eliminate lost travel time. Combine trips for errands. Clearly lay out a plan that considers how much running around you do. Instead of going grocery shopping in the morning and then taking things to the dry cleaner or stopping by your mother's house in the afternoon, combine the trips and save time and money while you're at it. If you have to run to the store for milk, make sure you take a quick look around to see whether there are other things you will need later for dinner. In my case, it takes me approximately fifteen minutes to get to the grocery store and the area where all the main shops are. That means in that round trip, I lose thirty minutes of my life driving (and possibly becoming aggravated by people who don't know how to drive). If I had to make two trips into town in one day, I would lose sixty minutes—time wasted. Done. Over. Why do that?

Outsource things. I lost tons of time doing things that I didn't like doing and didn't do well. If you can pay for lawn care, grocery shopping, or housecleaning, do it. There are so many other things you could be using that time for that you enjoy and that add value to your life. If you don't have the money to pay for things like that, try trading services with others. For example, if you don't like to garden but you love fresh veggies all summer long, try trading babysitting services with someone who likes gardening, or maybe try cooking meals for them to have in the freezer. There are lots of people who have the same dilemma as you. Get together and help each other out.

Shut down time bandits. We all know some time bandits in our lives. We even love many of them, which makes it that much more difficult to shut them down. It is necessary, though. For your own peace of mind and for the ability to accomplish more in your day, you must recognize them and shut them down.

Because we usually have more than one time bandit in our lives, it is conceivable to lose hours with people who drop in, call, or ask for help without any regard for what you might have planned. Don't spend hours on the phone talking to people when you don't want to hear about it all and have a million other things waiting for you to do. Don't do something with people if you don't enjoy spending time with them or if the timing isn't right. Don't be guilted into it. Don't let controlling people take over blocks of your time if it will not add value to your life.

Does that mean that you need to be rude and tell sweet Auntie Martha, who calls and keeps you on the phone for hours telling stories that you've already heard a hundred times, that you don't care about her and are not going to talk to her all day? Or does it mean you should tell your good friend that the last thing in the world you want to do is help her go through her closet to get rid of stuff? (After all, you have your own closet.) No. Does it mean that you tell your mom you would rather spend time painting your toenails and drinking a glass of wine than driving over to visit for an hour and listen to her recent run-in with a lady in the Walmart parking lot? Of course not.

There are kinder and gentler ways to do these things. Use tact and diplomacy, but take control. Maybe you can tell Aunt Martha that you are so happy to hear from her and look forward to seeing her in person soon. Then be sure to schedule a specific time to do that. Or set up times that are best for you to take calls. My grandfather used to talk with his brother every Sunday night at six. They both planned for that phone call to take place every week at that time, so they always had a clear calendar. No stress! You can decline helping your friend with her closet because of other obligations, but you should also tell her that you can't wait to get together for a movie on Friday night. And Mom? You can tell Mom almost anything as long as you dedicate a time to actually listen to and talk with her. You could probably even tell her the truth—that the kids are finally asleep, hubby is watching television, and you just need an hour of "me time." As a mom, she will probably get that. And as the old saying goes, it's not what you say but how you say it. It's about how you make people feel. But it is perfectly OK to control how you spend your time.

Choose activities wisely. Remember the Big Guilt Vacuum? Hear it coming and don't get sucked in. Don't spend time doing things that you don't want to do and don't have time to do. Don't be guilted into being on volunteer committees, baking for bake sales, watching other people's kids, helping others plan parties, or doing garage sales. Make a conscious choice about *how* to spend the limited time you have here on earth.

Learn to recognize when time is truly being wasted. It's OK to occasionally have some downtime, but when hours go by and you cannot name how that time added value to your life, it is usually accurate to consider it time wasted.

I used to spend hours on the road traveling to my next racing event, and for the longest time, I thought that I had no choice about losing all that time. It was out of my control because I had a commitment to be at the next racetrack. Wrong. I might have had to spend those hours on the road, but I didn't have to waste them. Instead, I found that to be a perfect time for continuing my online college course work, packaging and marketing items to sell, writing notes for an upcoming interview, or planning the next week's schedule and commitments. The bottom line was that I did have a choice. I just needed to recognize that and choose how best to use my precious time.

Infinity Factor #5: Purge. Eliminate time wasters.

R.U.S.H. REVIEW-Chapter 6: Purge

Chapter Highlights to Remember:

1. Don't waste precious time. Time spent is time you can never get back.
2. Be conscious of how you spend your time. It's your choice.
3. Identify and eliminate time wasters.

Start your own revolution! Ask yourself these questions to begin R.U.S.H.ing:

1. Do I ever wonder where the day went and realize that I wasted a lot of time with no real return on my investment?
2. Have I thought about how I really want to spend my time? Are there things that I could delegate to someone else or services that I could trade with someone?
3. What do I waste time on? What things could I eliminate from my life or spend less time on?

My R.U.S.H. vision for tomorrow:

I will

_____

_____

"I have everything under control," she said.
"It's all going according to plan."
"Of course," he said, as he cleaned up the mess she made.
"But next time could you choose a better plan?"

Seven

INFINITY FACTOR #6: PLAN AND PRIORITIZE—
ALWAYS SCHEDULE R.U.S.H. TIME

'm sure you've heard that scheduling your day is a surefire way to get the most accomplished, but do you realize that it doesn't apply just to your professional life, medical appointments, or social engagements? In today's crazy, fast-paced society, with its inherent need for work-life balance, learning to use a daily planner as part of a positivity ritual can be life changing in a good way.

First, you must understand the need to schedule, schedule, schedule everything, or it won't happen. You will never have the time if you don't make the time. Remember your goals, and schedule the tasks that will bring you closer to those goals. Schedule specific blocks of time to work on each of those tasks so that progress is continually made. It is also important to understand the need to prioritize the things that are most important to you and schedule those in first. I call this R.U.S.H. time—the things that are most important but are often ignored or overlooked, like me time.

For instance, in my crazy life, I have learned that there are three things that are extremely important to my well-being, and if they don't happen, I start to feel a negative effect. The first thing is my morning ritual, which consists of a thirty-minute workout and a chat with my husband before we both go to work. The second thing is family fun time with the kids. The third is an occasional date night with my hubby.

If any of those things fall by the wayside, I start to feel cranky and out of sorts. That tends to turn into feeling a bit depressed and unhappy. Not good. So I have learned to actually schedule date nights on the calendar twice a month. If it's on the calendar, it reminds me to make it happen and prompts me to make the necessary arrangements (dinner reservations and a babysitter), which locks it in. I also claim every Friday night as family fun night. My husband and I both know not to schedule anything else on Friday nights. It is reserved just for family time.

You might have different things that are most important to you. That's fine. The crucial thing is that you determine what those things are and then keep them as priorities in your life. Schedule that R.U.S.H. time.

Once you get into the routine of using a daily planner and getting your spouse or significant other to contribute to it also, it is essential to understand that all white space does not need to be used up. Just because a block of time on the calendar looks open doesn't mean that you need to fill it. Free time can also equate to me time. We all need time to recharge our batteries, run errands, watch TV, do crafts, wash our hair, work out, rest—whatever it is for you. It's OK to turn down invitations just to have time for yourself. Don't feel guilty. You are worthy and deserving of time for yourself. Remember, then, that when you see white space on the calendar, free time is me time, and me time is just as important as, and sometimes even more important than, anything else.

When I was racing the jet car at racetracks across the country, I not only didn't have much me time on the schedule but also had too many expectations from people, including myself, that I couldn't meet. I felt like I was spinning out of control. I was constantly on the go and constantly felt needed someplace, somewhere, whether it was because of a racing event or a situation at home. My racing boss had a completely different temperament than I did, so communication was sometimes difficult. Since we were together 24-7, it created some stress.

My racing fans stood in lines for hours waiting for me to autograph pictures or shirts for them, and I never wanted to disappoint them, so I spent many late-night hours after the racing was done trying to see them all, which cut down on my rest time. The lack of sleep created more stress. My weekly job at home left a lot to be desired. The norm was low pay, lots of hours, and a less-than-optimal working environment. Obviously, this just added more stress to my life. My family and friends felt like they never saw me enough, and since I was on the road a lot, I missed many important family events. I was always tired and feeling guilty about something. How wrong I was to feel that way!

A lot of what I learned during that time in my life contributed to me being the way I am today: confident, strong, and intentional in how I live. I became very aware that either I could control my life or my life would control me. I discovered the value of me time.

Here's a funny story about what happened to me at a racing event when I thought I was in control but perhaps was not. It was a hot, hot day at Maryland International Raceway. We had been waiting in line for hours to run a race, and I was exhausted.

Coming off of a day-long racing event in Englishtown, New Jersey, we had traveled all night, stealing a few winks of sleep in the cab of the truck when not on driving detail, to arrive at this track in Maryland in the wee hours of the morning. We ran to a hotel to grab a shower, a fresh set of clothes, and a coffee, and then we went straight to the track to prepare for the huge Jet Cars Under the Stars event at Maryland International Raceway. I was the featured driver there as the champion of the previous year's event and defender of my title.

We set up our racing pit area, I packed my parachutes, and I suited up to be ready to race. It was so hot that I was sweating profusely in my fire suit (safety gear). My mascara had melted off my eyelashes, my hair was hot and stringy, I was so tired it was hard to stay focused, and I really didn't feel that well, but I was a professional, so I said, "Nope. I can totally do this."

We spent the next eight hours running qualifying runs, and I really hadn't had any me time, as I had many responsibilities to attend to. People were counting on me. Then track officials told me that an ESPN reporter and camera crew were there and wanted to interview me at the end of the track after I ran the final race. ESPN! Woo-hoo! That was exciting! "No problem," I said. "See you at the end of the track."

Showtime came. I really wasn't feeling great, but the show must go on, and, of course, that ESPN interview would be so *cool!* My opponent and I started our cars and approached the starting line, and then nothing but pure adrenaline carried me the quarter mile to the finish line. I ran a 303-mph run in 5.24 seconds and won the race! I would continue my reign as champion of Jet Cars Under the Stars.

I slowed the car down at the end of the track, ecstatic to have won, but now I felt even worse. My crewman met me to take my helmet and realized that I was having difficulty getting out of the car. I was exhausted and weak. He lifted me out of the car and said, "The ESPN crew is over there. You don't have to do the interview if you can't. It's OK."

Are you kidding me? ESPN? I was totally not going to miss my interview just because I was feeling a little green around the gills. I puffed myself up and tried to shake my long, sweaty hair loose so that I looked carefree and cool instead of sweaty and sick. I waved to the ESPN reporter and camera crew. I think I got through two questions before I stopped talking, turned my head, bent over, and hurled everything that had been in my stomach on national TV. Oh. My. God.

Quite honestly, everyone was really great about it. I was mortified and could hardly stand up, but everyone was kind and immediately helped me get water and get back to my racing trailer so that I could lie down for a few minutes before accepting my trophy.

The reason I share this with you is because I can laugh about the whole thing now, and I can also totally see that I might have been able to control that whole scenario just a little bit better than I did. To begin with, our racing schedule plan should have included designated periods for what I call me time: time for rest, time for eating and hydrating, and time to tend to my body, mind, and soul. And if the plan didn't include it, I should have insisted on a change to the plan and scheduled that me time. But even after missing that opportunity to assert control, I should have recognized all the signs of dehydration and physical exhaustion and taken the actions necessary to correct the problems. Knowing that this was my job and therefore people were counting on me to fulfill certain responsibilities, I should have also prioritized what was most important and do those things first, adjusting some things to allow for that essential me time.

Plan and prioritize. It's not enough to just have a plan. It needs to be a good plan, and we should always prioritize the many things we need to do in our lives. That includes me time—R.U.S.H. time.

Infinity Factor #6: Plan and prioritize. Always schedule R.U.S.H. time.

R.U.S.H. REVIEW-Chapter 7: Plan and Prioritize

Chapter Highlights to Remember:

1. Schedule, schedule, schedule everything.
2. R.U.S.H. time is me time. Always schedule it. It should be a top priority.
3. Don't just have a plan—make sure it's a good one!

Start your own revolution! Ask yourself these questions to begin R.U.S.H.ing:

1. Do I have a calendar or planner on which I write down all my appointments and things that I need to get done?
2. Do I take a little time each day just for me? Do I feel like me time is important enough to schedule it on the calendar?
3. Do I make a plan for each day to ensure that everything that needs to get done and that I want to get done actually gets accomplished? Do I ensure that the plans I make are sensible, timely, and realistic?

My R.U.S.H. vision for tomorrow:

I will

_____

_____

"Who is that girl over there?" she asked. "She seems familiar somehow." She busied herself trying to rub the wrinkles away from the corners of her eyes. "That is the you before today," he said. "You are even more beautiful now."

Eight

INFINITY FACTOR #7: PROGRESS—
CONTINUALLY REINVENT YOURSELF

The seventh infinity factor is a simple one, but it is often forgotten or misunderstood. *Progress*, as I am using it here, is all about acknowledging and embracing the idea that we continually move forward in our life's journey each day. We don't really have a final destination that we want to get to, and we don't just stay the same forever. What we have is a way of life that continually changes and is altered as a result of our life's experiences and the choices that we make. That is where the joy is. It's truly in our life's journey. Our greatest joy can be found in intentionally living each day. It's about that moment at the end of each day when you feel satisfied that although everything may not be perfect, you made choices that were right for you that day as well as for the future.

My own priorities in life have changed in ways I never would have imagined. At age nineteen, when I was first embarking on the coolest, scariest, most amazing time of my life by driving a 300-mph jet car, my priorities and the choices I made were very different from those I make today. And that's OK, because I see things differently now. The things didn't change, but I did. I used to think nothing of traveling across the country every weekend between February and November to race, but now I have a family and I place family time ahead of a racing schedule. And although I used to easily accept the risk and danger of racing a 300-mph jet car, now I realize the impact that an accident would have on my children for the rest of their lives. Instead of feeling invincible and like I have my whole life ahead of me, I have experienced things that cause me to be very aware of how short life can be and how important it is to make every moment count. Continual growth and change are natural and good. We have an opportunity every morning to ask ourselves, "What do I want my life to be about today? What do I want to experience? Who do I want to be?"

Pin a bunch of labels on me, and at some point every one of them might be fitting. Sometimes I'm a mother, and sometimes I'm a wife. I'm a friend, a lover, a daughter, a sister, and a really lousy cook. I'm an organizer, a boss, a giver, a taker, an off-key singer, a dreamer, and the winningest jet car driver in US history. I'm a businesswoman, a fitness coach, a dog lover, a sap for silly love stories, a roller-coaster rider, a nice person, and a person who has doubts and uncertainties just like every other person in this crazy world. My label changes depending on what day it is and what mood I'm in, and often I wear more than one label at a time.

The most beautiful and treasured label I wear, though, is a simple one. I am Me—with a capital *M*. I am just me, and I am exactly who I want to be in every moment. Although that may not seem like a very special title and it is one that we all can claim, it is the most difficult label to wear and to be true to. That is mainly because I am often guilty of being a self-doubter. This is a tag that mysteriously appears and affixes itself to me when I least expect it. When I wear my self-doubter tag, there is no room for being me. When I wear my self-doubter tag, I'm not always even sure who the real me is. But through the power of R.U.S.H. and intentional living, I have learned to pay attention to the labels I wear, and if I don't like the one that's on me, I take action to change it—as simple as that. Each day I choose to be exactly who I want to be.

My life has changed and continues to progress because of the intentional choices that I make. Today the choices I make involve the well-being and desires of others besides just myself. I am a wife and a mama of three active little boys, who depend on me for so many things. My excitement about helping others to live a happier, more intentional life stemmed from my experiences back in my race car driving days of signing autographs and speaking at national events, but it continues to grow even now.

One of my most honored speaking invitations was for a racing sponsor, BIC Lighters, who asked me to speak at one of their national sales conventions. "Why in the world did they ask me to speak?" I had to ask myself, because I didn't think that many, if any, of their sales employees were race car drivers, and they certainly were not jet car drivers.

Their invitation opened my eyes to the fact that no matter what career choice each of us makes, we are all the same. To be successful at anything, we must intentionally make choices that will lead us to whatever type of success we desire, and we must take action. So with three hundred people watching, I walked up onto their sales convention stage and shared my story of racing success. I challenged those in the audience to be the very best they could be, not by magic but by specific design—by making a plan and taking action that could lead them to success and all of the benefits and self-happiness that success brings with it.

Making a decision to take action is the first proactive step in living a R.U.S.H. lifestyle through intentional living. Keep in mind that to get to the point of taking action, you probably have to be unhappy with something and perceive it to be a problem in your life, or you have to want something badly enough that you perceive *not* having it as a problem in your life. Either way, you want something to change. Doing nothing produces just that: nothing. Taking action is the only thing that will change your situation, so taking that first action step is significant. It's a positive step in the right direction.

The most important step, though, is evaluating the result of that action and then using what you learned to refine the action to more closely align with where you are headed—your goal. Look back to your personal mission statement and determine whether the action taken supports that statement. It's surprising how often, when we look back, we find that we were a bit off track right from the start. That's OK. Looking back to evaluate helps give us direction. So many people take this first action, evaluate the result, and then quit. It's over. They say, "Oh, it didn't work! I'm still not happy. I'm still not where I want to be." And they throw in the towel and cry.

All I can say is, "Wow!" When you're making a cake and you taste the batter and it's not sweet enough, do you just throw the whole thing out? No! You add more sugar and try again. That's what you do. You redirect and you continue to progress. And *that* is the secret for ending up where you want to be when taking actions in your life, especially when dealing with what you perceive to be issues or problems. You must take a deliberate action, evaluate it, and take another action—and another and another, if that's what it takes—until you eventually arrive where you want to be. It's all about self-awareness, progress, and continual advancement. Use this R.U.S.H. Progress Cycle chart to formulate an action plan for change.

Identify the Need for
Change (Problem)
(How do I feel now?)

Analyze
Progress
(Did the action
meet my need or
solve my
problem? If not,
repeat the
cycle.)

**R.U.S.H.
Progress
Cycle**

Identify
R.U.S.H. Goal

(How do I want
to feel?)

Implement New Action
(Select the best of all
possibilities
brainstormed.)

Brainstorm New
Actions to Take
(What can I do to make
myself feel better?)

Continually reinvent yourself using new knowledge you have gained and new life experiences you have lived. We cannot ever stay the same, because the nature of life is change. As hard as change can be to embrace sometimes, learning how to control it and having input to make the change good is a valuable tool in your tool kit of life. Although we may not be able to control all the variables that life throws our way, we do have the ability to take an active role in how we allow life to shape us and what we choose to take from it.

Every time I have had a change occur in my life that I was unhappy about, it has been beneficial for me to stop crying and complaining about it and try to decide how to move forward. There is always a time for crying and needing support, but then comes the time to lift our heads and decide just what it will take to make us feel better about it all. Be strong, and when that is hard for you, use your support system (R.U.S.H. buddies) to help carry the load until you can stand alone again.

Although some life events can leave us worn and scarred, we can learn from them and use the knowledge gained to move ourselves forward and to evolve into even better versions of ourselves. Continual reflection on who you are and who you want to be has the power to take you to your highest level of self-happiness and fulfillment.

Infinity Factor #7: Progress. Continually reinvent yourself.

R.U.S.H. REVIEW-Chapter 8: Progress

Chapter Highlights to Remember:

1. When life changes, you change. That's OK. Recreate. Reinvent. Evolve.
2. Use the R.U.S.H. Progress Cycle to help you make changes and resolve issues.
3. Embrace external change by taking an active role in how you allow it to shape you. Pull out your tool kit of life!

Start your own revolution! Ask yourself these questions to begin R.U.S.H.ing:

1. Do I periodically review my priorities in life? How often do I make changes to my goals and plans so that they accurately reflect the real me?
2. How do I make changes and resolve issues and problems in my life? Do I use a thorough approach to resolve them, or do I just put up with them and hope they go away on their own?
3. Have I ever quit too early when making a change or trying to resolve an issue? Do I try to embrace change, or do I let it negatively affect me without trying to make it a change for the better?

My R.U.S.H. vision for tomorrow:

I will

_____

_____

She smiled with the realization: "Winning in life is more about the race than it is the finish line."

Nine

Take the Win

Living life intentionally and with purpose leads to a happier and healthier life for you, but do you know what else it does? It creates a happier, healthier life for everyone around you as well. We are all connected. Family and friends who we know well are obviously affected by everything we say and do and every example that is set, but strangers are also affected. We have a great influence on all who come near us—coworkers, bosses, neighbors, shoppers at the mall, people in the grocery store, our kids' teachers, club members, people in restaurants, and so on. How we speak, how we dress, and how we behave all create the world we live in. People are affected, sometimes consciously and sometimes subconsciously, by our very presence.

Someone told me once that he really wanted to change the world but couldn't. Then he listed all the reasons why not. Among them were that he wasn't smart enough or educated enough and that he didn't have enough money. There were many more reasons. The thing he didn't really seem to understand was that everything we do changes the world. Although you might think that you are changing only your little part of the world, even one little change can change *the* world. Every little thing we do has an effect on someone or something, and the course of our lives is changed. We set an example with our daily behaviors, and other people notice. We need to remember the influence we have on everyone around us.

I was reminded of this in a few ways during my racing career. Since I was somewhat of a celebrity, I met and interacted with many different people in my travels. The fans who not only came to see me race but also waited in lines just to meet me and take a picture with me numbered in the thousands and stretched all across the United States and Puerto Rico. They were and still are a part of my heart, and I am humbled whenever I think back on those memories. For a while, I didn't understand how what I said or did might affect those fans. I just did the best job racing and appreciating my fans that I could. But I quickly found that who I was personally did have an effect on others, many times when I didn't even know it. I will share a few of those memories with you.

● ● ●

One evening when greeting fans at a Super Chevy show at Norwalk Raceway Park in Ohio, I was excited to share the joy of one couple who told me they were expecting a child. I had met Louisa Peck and Andre Brown Sr. the year before at a show, and I was happy to see them again and share in their good news. The following year, I was honored and awestruck when they brought their new baby daughter to meet me at the same racetrack and told me that they had named her "Jessica Susan" after me. After *me*! Why? Because they said that I had inspired them in a way no one had before, and they would be proud if their little Jessie could grow up and follow her dreams as I had. I was so humbled by this.

Jessie and Her Namesake, Jessica Susan Brown

• • •

I always loved interacting with fans, and so after one race I enjoyed meeting a young woman named Kristen who had come to the track with her brother, Mike. They waited in line for a long time to meet me, and when they finally got to the head of the line, Kristen had to nudge Mike to actually get a picture with me because he was so shy. In no time, though, we were all chatting and laughing together. They were young and fun, and I enjoyed meeting them. Mike specifically thanked me for taking the time to meet him.

Two months later, I was shocked to receive a message from Kristen explaining that her brother had been in an accident and had suffered a serious trauma to his brain. He was in a coma. She asked if she could post the picture I had taken with Mike on a website she had created to post progress reports and prayers for him. She said that the picture was special to him. I remembered both of them without a doubt, and of course, I said yes. My heart ached for Mike and his family, and I continued to stay in contact, even visiting.

Mike defied the odds and came out of that coma. They told me that when he looked at our picture, at first he didn't know who I was and asked if I was his girlfriend. As his memory returned to him, he realized that I was "the race car girl." After months of recovery and rehabilitation, we reunited at the Cleveland Auto-Rama in Ohio. My heart practically stopped when he looked at me with his eyes wide and said, "I remember you!" I still thank God for this miracle of continued life. Mike is strong and healthy today, and I feel a bond with him and his family that I am positive can never be broken. He will never be far from my heart.

Jessie with Mike Gamauf

• • •

Twelve-year-old Erika Harvey and her dad, Wylie Frank, watched me make history by winning a world championship at my very first race, and she was my first and my number-one fan. After meeting me after a show, they followed me to many different racetracks, helping me whenever they could by setting things up and selling T-shirts, bringing me water when it was hot out, meeting my family, and staying in touch with me for fourteen years and counting. Erika has grown into such a beautiful young woman, and she says that I made a difference in her life—a positive difference. I am blessed to still be part of her life.

Jessie with Her Number-One Fan, Erika Harvey

• • •

There have been many different young female racers who have contacted me to tell me that they met me at the racetrack when they were little and that I was their inspiration to eventually drive a race car. One of those little girls grew up to be a jet car driver just like me and went on to drive the very same car that I did. Sarah Edwards, from Stamford, Connecticut, said that at twelve years old, she saw me race, met me, and told her parents, "That's what I want to do." And she did. She drove her own race car and developed the skills she needed to get into the field. And then—and I consider this to be the most significant thing she did—she introduced herself to the jet car team that she wanted to race with and told them, "I want to race." She now races the same Hanna Motorsports Queen of Diamonds jet car that I did. What a great example of someone recognizing her dream and going on to set goals and take the action necessary to make her dream come true. Knowing that I was an inspiration to her makes me very proud.

● ● ●

Recognizing that I truly had an effect on people made me realize how precious life is and how serious our responsibilities to others and the world are. Remember that your influence reaches far, even without your conscious awareness, and it will be either a good influence or a bad one. It is your choice.

Embrace change instead of being afraid of it. Create change to find self-happiness instead of waiting for something beyond your control to bring happiness to you. This mind-set can be revolutionary if you are strong and intentional about the life you wish to live.

Although I started out racing a jet car and focusing on the finish line to win races, I ended up learning that it wasn't all about the finish line on the track. It was about the incredible journey of my life and all the people I was blessed to share it with. My life purpose became clear during my journey, and that purpose wasn't in winning the race with a drag car. It was how my racing, winning, and influence affected others in a positive way.

My journey continues today; I spend much of my time working with others to help them rev up their self-happiness by owning it. I still love racing and occasionally make some runs down the track. I still love interacting with people, and social media has made that easier than ever. I love my business and my family. I love my life and the journey that I'm on, and *that* is winning to me.

Enjoy your journey. "R.U.S.H. on," and take *your* win. It is yours for the taking.

Jessie Harris Bouton: "R.U.S.H. On!"

R.U.S.H. REVIEW-Chapter 9: Take the Win

Chapter Highlights to Remember:

1. Live life intentionally to enjoy a happier, healthier life.
2. Remember the influence you have on everyone you come in contact with.
3. Embrace change, and take your win. It is waiting for you.

Start your own revolution! Ask yourself these questions to begin R.U.S.H.ing:

1. Have I taken the time to learn enough about myself to make choices that truly make me happier and more content with my life?
2. What did I do today that had an impact on someone else? Was it a positive or a negative impact? Is there anyone whose life I influenced without really knowing it at the time? How?
3. Do I embrace change in my life and know it to be natural and good?
4. Do I value myself enough to know that I am deserving of my Best Life Ever? Do I understand that the concept of revving up my self-happiness isn't just about me, because it creates a better life for all those around me as well?
5. Am I ready to take my win?

My R.U.S.H. vision for tomorrow:

I will

_____

_____

About the Author

Jessie Harris Bouton, CEO of Infinity Wellness, public speaker,
trainer, life and fitness coach, wellness and success strategist

Jessie is a former professional race car driver and legend in the sport of drag racing as the winningest jet car driver in history. Following her seven-year racing career, she became a wife and mother but eventually felt that she wanted more in her life. Seeking to rev up her own self-happiness, she used the art of intentional living to create a life that she loves.

Chosen as a Zonta International Woman of the Year in Rome, New York, Bouton was also a nominee for inclusion in the Rome Sports Hall of Fame. She holds an associate's degree in liberal arts and works tirelessly to raise awareness of the importance of organ donation.

She lives with her husband, three sons, and favorite pup, Daisy, in Upstate New York.

To learn more or to contact Jessie, go to www.infinitywellness project.com.

Made in the USA
Charleston, SC
20 January 2017